Finding My Way Back

Nicole Smolinski

Prologue, a note to my readers:

Recently I found an old letter, written from my mom, addressed to me. She wrote it when I was young, hoping I'd find it years later. In that letter, she described a bright little girl who included so many different people to play and wouldn't ever choose favorites. A little girl who had gotten into an argument because someone had insulted her friend. A little girl who believed in herself, believed in her journey, and made a point of taking others along with her to live it. A little girl that I didn't quite recognize anymore when I looked in the mirror.

I think elementary-school-me was far braver than I am now — I am fighting to get back to my elementary school self. I am fighting to retrieve all of the parts of me that were lost or stolen or ripped off along the way.

I would like this collection to be for anyone who has or continues to question their worth and their purpose in the world. If you're reading this, take heart. This is tough. I don't know who you are, if you're young and just starting out — journeying to be okay with yourself in a harsh world — or if you've already spent years weighed down by the journey. From my own experience, I've seen people ranging all ages still asking the world if they are enough. My hope is to empower readers to take their worth into their own hands — to transition from allowing others to tell them who they are to boldly defining that for themselves. To take back their lives.

And so today, I share my own journey with you. I am humbled and excited and terrified to do so. As you continue reading, you'll bear witness to the internal seasons I've walked through over the years. I must have lived at least ten years in my winter, before any spring awakening began in me. In reality, though, my process was not so clean cut. There is no "pain" or "glory" section of life, no "good" section or "bad." They are all one and the same, so tightly interwoven with one another that they're simply impossible to tease out. I want you to know that healing is rarely linear. Mine certainly isn't. I have learned the same lessons, multiple times, in different ways. Just as winter folds into spring, my pain and joy fold into each other all year long. Maybe one day, I'll fully understand. Probably not.

Through so much of the pain, I've come to accept and appreciate that healing most often comes in the form of spirals more than straight lines. I am learning to welcome the return of life's most important lessons, just as I welcome my return to self. I hope you'll join me.

With joy,

Nicole

Contents

For everyone who's lost themselves, in some way or another.
And for you, little one.
You were so brave. Proud of you.

It's daunting to see how different I was as time went on.
It all happened so slowly and smoothly,
I didn't even realize so much of me
had slipped out the back door.
Like a pick pocketer,
smooth and seamless,
you don't realize you've lost yourself
until much later.

I. Winter

Winter often looks barren because the flowers don't grow, but I've learned winter is anything but barren—seedlings wait to sprout underground when the time comes and the environment is ready. I believe winter is our teacher because all the outward, beautiful stuff falls away for awhile and we're left with only our core. Winter isn't showy like spring, but it is wise and humble. Of course, it's way more fun to be blooming and radiant, but spring doesn't come without a winter of strengthening our roots. It's my honor to be tested, to be stripped, because my roots are revealed and it's only then that I can realign myself in better soil. I thank the harsh winter for what it's taught me, and I wait expectantly for spring to come.

When People Tell Me, "It's Only Because He Loves You"

For as long as I can remember,
people have been pointing to the hand
that continually slaps me across the face;
they point, and they label it love.
And I caress my cheek,
wondering why this thing they call love

stings so badly.

Nicole Smolinski

Can people create their own demons?
Or perhaps just create a safe place
for them to be housed.
Because I'm almost certain I've created mine,
or made a damn good hostess in the least.

Tell me:
When did luxury become necessity,
Kindness a bribe,
Status a priority,
Compassion a hobby?

Nicole Smolinski

We are often our own worst enemy.
I've gone my whole life
dying to be loved by people,
yet I've never even given myself
permission to be loved.

Finding My Way Back

Cells are programmed to attack
what's unknown to them —
different, not one of us.
But there's a disease
where cells think their own
are not like them,
and they attack.

In medicine we call it autoimmunity,
but sometimes I think we should just call it
the human condition.

Nicole Smolinski

The cycle

Words pour out of your mouth
and I can never tell
whether, for today,
the liquid will be
medicine
or poison.

Finding My Way Back

How is it
that when I cry out to you, God,
all I hear are the echoes of my own cries?
Like the Grand Canyon of sorrows.
Like clanging repetitions—
reminding myself of my desperation—
over and over
until they're replaced by silence
in the canyon once more.

Nicole Smolinski

There are days when I feel like
my life is a big city alley mugging.
People sit in their apartments above, listening to me
scream;
passersby catch glimpses as they cross the alley,
watching for only a second
until they continue along their journey.
Scared of what will happen if they don't get involved
but more scared about what will happen if they do.
So they continue on,
and I pray for help as I'm pushed to the ground,
wondering why I see people all around me
and not one has come to see
if I may need someone
to pull these demons off my body.

House Repairs

Today my eyes ache from carrying all its luggage.
Today I keep trying to reach the plumber
so he can fix the leak in my eyes
but he can't seem to return my calls.
Today I cannot wear a smiley mask
because I seem to have misplaced it
in all the mess.

Therapy

I dread the mornings
when I have to sit and stare
at my life for too long.
Like a photo of myself,
the longer I stare
the more inadequacies I seem to notice...
all the blemishes and bumps and bruises,
until my whole self in its entirety
seems ugly.

Finding My Way Back

That day, the world slowed down
and I began to understand
that life continually presents you with middles.
It is never simple.
I sat there wishing for a black and white world.

How unfair, that you bring the black
but can only see the white in yourself?

Nicole Smolinski

Keeping Busy

I am tired,
And I wonder why my answer to exhaustion
is to run more.
But then I remember,
that when I try to stop,
to rest,
to catch a breath,
my demons catch up with me.
The thoughts I was escaping from
close the gap
and enter my mind once more.
Telling me I am nothing,
tormenting my every second.
So I continue running,
because it's the only way to escape the noise.

Finding My Way Back

Dear Maker:

Excuse me, hello.

Yes, I'm calling about a technical difficulty I've been
having.
You see, my wires aren't working like they should be.
Good company is shared with me and yet I feel more
alone.
Love is given and I feel sadness.
Some things must be mixed up in there,
some wires crossed, maybe.
I'm not quite sure how else to describe the problem
but I'm certain this isn't right.
I am looking at the manual and it doesn't match up.
Maybe I was made wrong from the start,
or maybe things got all tangled along the way.
Anyhow, when you get the chance,
can you stop by and fix me?
It's beginning to hurt a little too much.

Thank you in advance.

Nicole Smolinski

The scar will heal,
but it will never go away.
So will I never be able to forget
what you've done to me.

In Another Life

I was gasping for air for so long
suffocating
that my body grew lungs.
But instead of joining others underwater,
I had to stay ashore.
So I learned how to breathe differently than everyone
else
separated by the ways I learned to survive in another
life.

Nicole Smolinski

Gone

They take a small part of me each time they go,
and they always seem to come back wanting more.
The worst part is, each time,
I don't know how to say no.
Piece by piece,
I disappear.
I am no more.

Finding My Way Back

Knowledge is not enough.
I've seen too many intelligent people
who have the sword of the kingdom in their hands
but do not know how to wield it.

Nicole Smolinski

Crooked Love

I think back to my young self,
and I can remember how trapped she was.
How confused and hurt and angered.

I am a woman now.
A woman that doesn't really know
how to be cared for,
to be challenged,
to be protected,
or to be touched.
When someone wants me, I fear it'll be too much.
And when someone doesn't, I fear I'm not enough.

I spent years adapting to a crooked love system
and now,
I don't really know how to love straight.

Now and Then

Every now and then,
I look up at my race
and I notice I'm behind where I should be.
I think back to all of those times
where I wanted to run,
to stay on track.
But you held me back by the collar
and you called it love.

Now years later
all I'm left with
is a stretched out t-shirt
and a life laps behind where I could have been.

II. Spring

Spring is for hope,
for slow growth
and rising up.

A celebration, of sorts

Today is a celebration —
because today is the day things get better.
Today is the day I hit rock bottom,
which means there's only up to go from here.
Today is a somber backwards twisted celebration.
Because I simply have to believe
life can't possibly do anything
except get better.

Nicole Smolinski

A reminder to my future self

Remember that you were calm.
Remember that you were honest.
Remember that you admitted hurt.
Remember that they continued to blame you,
continued to say they didn't mean it,
or that the words just came out wrong.
Remember that, after you gave up everything for them,
they still looked you in the eye
and said, "not enough."
Remember that they tried to make you feel inadequate.
Remember that they tried to make you feel guilty.
Most of all, remember that they tried to take
your feelings, your opinions, your hurts, your mind,
and make them nothing.
Remember that it's all bullshit.
Remember that you are stronger.

Finding My Way Back

I don't know how to feel angry or sad
without guilt and weakness following suit.
Grace flows like a waterfall
even for those who've hurt me so deeply
but the streams run dry
when I attempt grace towards myself.

Parts of me still scream
that I must have done something
to deserve this life.

Nicole Smolinski

How does a soul find comfort?
Because some days life seems too unfair to be real.
Some days my heart breaks so badly for my wounded
soul
that my brain wrenches at the thought of it.
Some days my body aches
at the impossible attempt to hug what's inside of me.
And my soul thanks them for their efforts,
recognizing that they're doing their best—
that the collective "me" is doing my best—
but knowing deep down that some days
the only way to comfort the soul
is to hope for a better tomorrow.

Finding My Way Back

Maybe
if the sun can rise again
each morning,
I can too.

Maybe
if the sun can
rise again
each morning,
I can too.

Finding My Way Back

Is it naive or faithful to desire the things of Heaven,
knowing full well we are not living amongst the angels?
Instead broken, cruel, lost...
A little of both, I suppose.

Nicole Smolinski

Esther

What do you do when you know it's your time,
but you don't want it to be?
When you've been waiting and hoping for this big
moment,
for this breakthrough.
But when it's right in front of your face,
it looks a lot uglier close up,
your obstacles.
There is more to see and features much more defined.
You're now so close you can smell its rancid breath.
What do you do then?
This moment you've been preparing for is finally here,
and you remember that you're scared.
But what you cannot do is look away.
This is the moment.
The moment where you buckle down,
look your monster straight in his biting, ravenous
eyes…
In all his horror.
And you press on.
Letting him know that even though you're scared,
you will not let him steal your courage.
Because this is your moment
Into freedom.

Finding My Way Back

Morning Routines

When you're young, you're taught a morning routine
that usually involves brushing your teeth, getting
dressed, preparing a balanced breakfast for yourself.
No one told me I'd have to set aside time to unpack my
burdens every morning— to set everything down before
me and stare at the life I am living and will continue to
live when I walk out my front door.
No one told me to add these things to my morning
routine.

So I wake up, I brush my teeth and I get dressed.
Sometimes I even make myself a nice breakfast. But
mostly, I wake up and remember that my normal is not
what it should be. That I have to relearn how to love
and be loved. I have to re-forgive every single day and
mourn for my own broken heart.
As I head to the front door, my morning routine
finished, I make sure not to forget a handful of hope to
bring with me as I step outside for the day.

Tomorrow will look the same, and I'll muster up a new
handful to carry with me.
This is what mornings truly look like.

Pain is an old friend of mine.
We became acquainted very early on
and we just always seem to run into each other
wherever I go.
Pain is that friend that's seen me change over the years
and sticks around through it all.
I guess you could say pain is a pretty close friend of
mine.
The good news is, pain is a close friend to most people
in some way or another.
It is that mutual friend that breaks the ice,
it is the handshake of the soul.
So I've tried to see pain as a difficult but dear friend
rather than a foe,
because it has given me connection
with everyone I've come to meet.

Finding My Way Back

Take this cup from me

Everyone glorifies courage
but no one ever talks about
how difficult courage really is.

Nicole Smolinski

On saying no

I see your arm in motion.
A nasty right hook
lands right where it's always aimed
and my heart cracks once more
from the impact.

Time after time,
I let it break me.

And when I finally gather the courage
to block your fist,
when I finally decide
that one more crack
may cause my heart to shatter,
guilt washes over me.

How can this be?
That somehow I feel like the monster
for not wanting
to be hurt anymore.

Finding My Way Back

Things don't have to stay the same
One of the biggest lies might just be
that we cannot change.
That nature takes precedent over nurture.
That what's in our blood will always be.

We have a say in our own lives.
In the very same way I get up in the morning
and decide on cereal or toast,
I can decide who I'm going to be.

Nicole Smolinski

I often waiver in my thoughts
on whether humans are innately good or bad –
but what I do not waiver on
is the fact that we can surely become better.

The process

I am learning it's okay to say I'm not ready yet —
there is still work to do.

I am learning
it's OK to say
I'm not ready yet —
there is still
work to do.

Finding My Way Back

I am so afraid of brokenness. I sit here torn because I can see where things could be better if the roots I lived on were stronger, but knowing for that to happen I'd need to cut down the entire plant. And knowing full well that it's a lot easier to live on weak roots as long as you know what it gets you rather than tearing it all down to seek the hopefully better but mostly unknown alternative.

In forestry, there's a concept known as prescribed burn, where a wildfire is intentionally set for forest management. It's conducted to clear buildup and decrease likelihood of serious hotter fires that are less contained. Some cones, like the Sequoia, require heat from fire to open the cones and disperse seeds.

The forest has taught me that maybe we shouldn't be so afraid of brokenness if we're intentional about what we do with the inevitability of a broken life. I'd rather let the fires of my unhealthy hurts burn if it means regrowth can begin. Without this fire, without letting myself come freely undone and feel all of my pain, nature tells us that a greater fire will start— one of anger, bitterness, resentment. One of shutting down or lashing out.

I'm starting to look at brokenness differently, allowing it to do its full work in me. So that this fire can burn all the shrubs in my soul that are sitting on top of the fruitful cones. The cones that need to find the heat of the healing fire to spark regrowth.

In the brokenness, what is useless and painful clears away. And we can start anew.

Nicole Smolinski

Mirror, mirror

I see people trying their best,
I see people believing they're not good enough,
I see people looking left and right in comparison,
Rather than straight ahead.

I take one last look at the mirror,
and turn away until tomorrow morning.
I touch the mirror in front of me.
I see all of the these people around me,
And in them, I see myself.

Finding My Way Back

Wait up

We are remarkable beings.
Constantly changing, always in motion.
So much so that I often find my own brain
trying to catch up with itself...
trying to catch up with all the work
my soul's been doing all on its own.

Nicole Smolinski

Sometimes giving our delicate, bandaged hearts
back to the unpredictable world
is the bravest thing we can do.

Sometimes giving
our delicate,
bandaged hearts
back to the
unpredictable world
is the bravest thing
we can do.

Nicole Smolinski

Before a single tear can even finish its journey
down my cheek,
I feel my body contract in rejection.
I feel my tongue start to form the words
to excuse my inappropriate behavior.
I feel my throat clench up tight
trying to stop the sound of pain
from exiting my body.
I hear my brain sending waves and synapse responses
telling me I am completely overreacting.
I feel my hand instinctually wipe my face,
hiding the evidence.

Every part of me has been trained to reject the idea
that expressing pain is an option.

Lately, as my tear continues to fall,
I am trying to hone in
on the tiny rumble inside of me saying,
"Hey, let's stay here for a moment."
I think it is my soul,
trying to let me heal rather than ignore.
Trying to fight its way back
into the conference room of my self.
Trying to have a say again.

Vermin

Fear is a funny thing.
It creeps up on you
just when you think you've conquered it.
Right when you've gotten comfortable,
when you allow yourself to breathe,
it's back to haunt you all over again.

The worst demons we face are often like that.
They don't just get defeated and disappear overnight;
instead, they hide under the surface
and take on a new form
when we're just getting comfortable
in our own skin again.

I am plagued by fear,
but I am also plagued by big dreams…
maybe they always come in a package deal like this.

Finding My Way Back

To my therapist

Damn.
All I can feel
is fear
and there you are
calling it courage.

Nicole Smolinski

Nothing quenches the thirst
in your drought-stricken morale
quite like a raindrop of hope.

Finding My Way Back

Should I just give up

Is it naive to believe that "better" is out there?

What happens when your dreams
are bigger than your current reality?
Where do you put all those big dreams
taking up space in your head?
Do you stow them away,
do you throw them away?
How will you ever know
if you'll be able to use them one day?
Are they like that tool you'll be able to use at a later
time,
that shirt you'll grow into in a little while?
Or are they more like those little trinkets you never
touch
but can't seem to get rid of?
The ones that keeps taking up space
where other things,
perhaps more realistic ideas,
could be.

How do we de-clutter our dreams
when all of them seem so dear to us at the time?

Nicole Smolinski

Labels

We never dream bigger than what's comfortable
and label it strategy.
We let fear drive our decisions
and label it security.
We wait for permission to take risks
and label it patience.

Finding My Way Back

Start
with
      anger,
           frustration,
                  sadness,
                        sure.

But
always, always
end
with

                  hope.

Grieving the loss of the life
you'd imagined for yourself
is the first step towards
living an unimaginable life.

Grieving the loss
of the life
you'd imagined
for yourself
is the first step
towards living an
unimaginable life.

Nicole Smolinski

Out of the dust

Words have not always been good to me.
But I am dusting myself off.
I am taking the nasty sentences that were strewn
together
and thrown at me all those years,
breaking them apart,
and rearranging their letters
into something beautiful.

Finding My Way Back

Frustration is a natural emotion, like an organic fruit in the garden. But if you let it sit for too long, if you do not tend to it and nurture it into hope, it will muster and rot in your soul until it is something much uglier and less useful: resentment.

Resentment, much like rotten fruit, is not meant to nourish your body and soul. Be attentive to how you tend your Garden. Hope is like water— necessary for the best fruit during your harvest.

Be attentive to how
you tend your Garden.
Hope is like water—

necessary for
the best fruit
during your harvest.

Finding My Way Back

What if maybe
just maybe
I am already the person
I believe I can be?

What if she is already inside of me,
and always has been,
simply waiting to be reawakened?

Nicole Smolinski

Sometimes I feel like life is suffocating me — in deadlines, meetings, standards, not-enoughs. Doing things is hard enough and doing them well is a whole other challenge. But then I realize the more I see life as full of obligations, I take away the daily joys. It turns out it's not life who is suffocating me... I am suffocating myself. I cover myself up in the "have-to" mindset. Now more than ever, I'm seeing the value of living a get-to life rather than a have-to life. I unwrap myself from obligation. Undone, I uncover a life of opportunity.

Finding My Way Back

When did I become convinced
that my life belongs
to anyone but myself?

When did I become convinced that my life belongs to anyone but myself?

Finding My Way Back

Today I want a nice, strong pull of espresso. A whiskey neat rather than a cocktail. In fact, I want the strong stuff in all aspects of life. I don't want to do anything halfway. I don't want a life that coddles me with artificial and temporary sweetness, even though it's much easier to swallow in the moment. I crave the taste of real, raw life in a world that's constantly trying to convince us to be content with an average one. One that can be a little bitter sometimes. But the bitterness is oddly satisfying because it's genuine. Today I challenge life to give me the real stuff— because I know I can take it. Because I know I have people who want to challenge me and grow alongside me. Growing pains are called pains for a reason, but the more you grow into your own skin, the closer you find yourself to feeling at home. The more you embrace the promise that leaning in will get you closer to freedom, the more you dare to grow. And that's worth every bitter sip that life has to offer.

Nicole Smolinski

I like to look back at things
that would have crushed me years ago
but instead simply vibrate the steady ground
I now stand upon.

Finding My Way Back

The day I was free from you, I didn't feel free.

The day I was free from you, I wasn't really free.
I had stepped out of your chains and picked up new ones.
Locked myself in fear, shame and self-hatred.
Maybe that was your plan all along.

And so I built my own prison after escaping yours.
And I called it home, believing this freedom
wasn't much better than what I had before.

The day I was really free from you, I was free from myself, too.
The day I was free was the day I embraced the fear
instead of drowning in it,
the day I accepted you for your faults and me for mine.
The day I looked at myself in the mirror hard enough
to realize there were shackles tied around my ankles,
and they no longer had your name on them,
but my own name instead.

That is when I said no more.
I glanced at myself in the reflection again,
and for the first time ever, I smiled back at her.
My strong and aching, pained and powerful body.
"You have survived the worst", I said. "It's time to let go."
And I bent down, and unlocked myself from the past.

That was the day I felt free.

Nicole Smolinski

I think of how the world has continued to beat and bruise me, so much so that there are parts of my heart left completely raw. But I am grateful, because the world has done me an unexpected favor. The world has given me a tender heart— one that is available and intentional, vibrant and aware, one that can connect with others in their own pain. So I laugh at the world's efforts, for each time it has tried to make me weak it unknowingly continues to make me strong.

So I laugh at the world's efforts, for each time it has tried to make me weak it unknowingly continues to make me strong.

Nicole Smolinski

A lot of days I fight off the idea that I am only lovely at a distance; like a pristine, collectible doll on the shelf, beautiful to look at but not really exciting enough to play with. I used to think I had to sit and wait for someone to open up the box and let me out into the engaging world. Lately, I'm breathing in the sweet air that comes with liking who I am and who I'm becoming. Lately, I'm starting to realize my packaging has never been glued shut, even when I believed it to be. Now I see that I can step outside whenever I want, even though it's scary. Scary and confusing and freeing and incredible. Maybe this is how Pinocchio must have felt, arms wooden and cold turning into warm flesh stretching out to reach the vast world, plastic, glazed eyes now blinking wide to see all I've been missing. Maybe this is what opening my box is, slowly but surely tearing off the hazy veil that's been in front of me all these years, telling me I'm not enough to play a part in the real world; maybe this is what becoming feels like. I think I like it.

III. Summary

Summer is for embrace
Taking what has been in process
And grasping it all,
Soaking it up,
Living in it fully.

Finding My Way Back

The only thing that terrifies me more than my dreams is who I'll be if I don't pursue them.

The only thing that
terrifies me
more than my dreams
is who I'll be
if I don't pursue them.

Finding My Way Back

Distance feeds fear. A lot of times our fears look like terrifying, dark monsters in the distance. And it's only when we lean in— get the courage to move closer, shine some light on them— that we see the monster was really nothing but an oddly-shaped bush or a weird shadow the entire time... and we move past it, softly laughing at ourselves for getting so worked up.

Nicole Smolinski

Reserve Tank

I've found that anger is far more draining than grace,
so I cannot comprehend how our world
is not completely and utterly empty?
It brings me joy to think
this can only mean there is a reserve tank —
made up of people still choosing grace,
keeping the world from exhaustion.

Finding My Way Back

You were strong before you believed in your strength.
You were worthy before you believed in your worth.
Change begins when you believe,
but that does not mean
it was never there in the first place...
You cannot see the fuel until it is ignited into flame.

Nicole Smolinski

I went on a challenging hike the other day, and I didn't even make it to the top. I kept staring at the people who made it up, jealous and competitive but knowing that it was too windy for me to try and climb the increasingly uneven rocks. I even hit my head trying. You see, when I first started the steps were paved and the climb was easy. But the closer I got to the top, the harder it was.

I think living a True life is a lot like that; not because it's necessarily hard to get there, but because the closer I get to living a life that represents what I think Heaven looks like, the more I'm challenged — my own human nature tempts me to give up, take the easy route, be selfish, the list is endless.

Even so I think God enjoys our process, celebrates our climb, and says it's okay that we haven't made it to the top yet as long as we're not constantly looking up at others and comparing their journeys to ours. The thing about moving closer to Heaven is that it's really challenging, but the higher I get the better the view.

So I worked my way up and enjoyed every minute, and I swear I felt the breeze usher me up when I got most tired. That day I was reminded that God is cheering at every step in our lives, a gust of breeze flowing out of His mighty mouth with each cheer... even when you bump your head a little. Here's to learning.

Finding My Way Back

Grace is the transformative power.
The refining fire of the Jewelry-Maker
that burns a little under the pressure
as your impurities and hurts burn away
but somehow warms your soul in the process.
And before you know it,
you've been molded anew.
Before you know it,
you're beautiful, shining gold.

Nicole Smolinski

We spend our lives believing
that it's all about this search
for belonging,
when it's really about this realization
that we've belonged all along.

Finding My Way Back

I read that our brains organize our memories and
experiences into a story,
known as our personal narrative.

In your life full of inevitable highs and lows, do you see
your lows following your highs… ruining what was
good? Or do you see your highs following your lows…
bringing redemption? The truth is, objectively, the
outcomes of our timeline are the same. We cannot
change the past.

We will never know the chicken-egg answer, whether
our highs or lows come first in this fluent thing called
life. Our history may not change — but our theme will,
based on how we choose to tell our stories. And how we
see our stories changes everything about how we see
the world, how we interact with the world. In fact, I'd
even argue that it will change our futures.
What's the theme of your life?
(Because I'm sure as hell choosing redemption).

Be the constant for people in an unstable world.
That is the superpower of mankind.

Be the constant
for people in an
unstable world.
That is the
superpower of
mankind.

Nicole Smolinski

There's something to be said about keeping your heart open. There is pain and rejection and it doesn't always work out like you planned it...
But it is vibrant.
Yes, a life lived wide open is vibrant and lively and exciting, intentional and unexpected.

Finding My Way Back

Reach. Reach for the greater. For the scary stupid dreams that seem so big you don't even know how they got placed in your little head. They call out to you, urging you to take up the challenge. And how do you respond?

Lift. Lift your hands up to surrender— to goodness, to unfathomably and undeservingly huge faith, to grace when your journey towards those dreams doesn't always go as planned.

Suddenly, fear falls away. Insecurities chip off of you like wax cracking off skin. Lift it all up and give it away and you will be uplifted in return. Life is just funny that way.

Nicole Smolinski

**That one quote, "When you realize just how perfect
everything is you will tilt your head back and laugh at
the sky"**

I believe in the power of a moment...
That when you focus on this exact moment before you,
existing just now, all is well.
Life is absolutely perfect, just then.
And there's rest and there's freedom.

Finding My Way Back

One of my most faithful reminders of worth is nature herself. In the same way a flower cannot exist without the bee, you cannot disappear without impacting the world in some way. These intricacies of nature do not have me worried about life's fragility, but rather encourage me in my own worth in this big, complicated universe. For I have my own flowers that are affected by me, and my own bees of whom I'm equally affected by. And together, we find belonging.

Nicole Smolinski

It is a treasure to find places that allow me
to finally set up camp in my own skin.

Finding My Way Back

We jump

               and let our steps
form under us

                  as we go.

Choose to care. Chase dreams that scare you. Dare to try. Dare to fail. Dare to look a little stupid. Laugh about it. Take notes on what you've learned. Continue on. Just don't ever for a second accept a sideline life for yourself.

Choose to care. Chase dreams that scare you. Dare to try Dare to fail. Dare to look a little stupid. Laugh about it. Take notes on what you've learned. Continue on. Just don't ever for a second accept a sideline life for yourself.

Nicole Smolinski

Do not let the world numb you.
When we allow our hearts to break
for those who have been through tragedy—
for those who can't afford to let theirs fully collapse—
we take a little of their burden,
share a little of their pain,
and that is how we begin to collectively mend.

I know we all desire this "perfect love." The award-winning, dramatically romantic kind.

But doesn't it say more that we are incapable of such unreachable love and are trying our best anyways? That we're fully aware there's no manual or handbook, but are showing up every day doing our best to love the best way we know how... even though it doesn't always turn out smooth or how we'd want it to. It's easy to follow a manual.

It takes guts— *real* love, I might even say— to realize you have no idea how to love well and show up, ready to try, anyways.

Nicole Smolinski

I find the greatest joy when storytelling.
Pay attention, listen often.
Our best teachers are often the normal people
sitting amongst us
trying to figure out life like we are.

Pay attention,
listen often.

Nicole Smolinski

Why do we all stand around pretending to be flawless
when we know full well how beautifully human it is
to not be?

Finding My Way Back

The most impactful thing we can do in a world
that's inclined to dehumanize
is welcome people to feel human again,
to return to themselves.

Nicole Smolinski

The other day, I scanned the beach for shells to take home for my friends. As I picked each one up off the sandy ground, I felt excited about giving it a new home, a new purpose.

When we finish seasons in our lives and are forced to start new ones, I guess we're all kind of like shells, washed up by the waters into the unknown. And it's new and scary and you don't know how you'll find your life or if anyone will want you to be a part of theirs. But we wait with patience and hope amongst all the others until God picks us up and gives us a new purpose.

That's the coolest part about the journey we're on — the minute we conquer a dream God gives us the opportunity to go catch another one. To go get lost in the exhilarating waves and wash up on some other beautiful beach, waiting to discover yet another part that lies within you.

Finding My Way Back

I feel most alive when the wind chill cuts through my cheek bones, turning them stiff and rosy without hindering the corners of my lips from turning upwards into a soft smile; when the music plays loud, challenging my lungs to burst out the lyrics louder than the speaker can, as if this will somehow allow their words to become my own; when the air around me carelessly blows through my tangled hair and my brain isn't thinking about how messy it looks or anything except how fully alive we can be when we're able to recognize these unexpected moments are magic before they are over with.

how fully alive we can be

when we're able to recognize

these unexpected moments

are magic

before they are over with

Some days I want to be big when God has created me to be small. I want to walk into rooms and turn heads and excite people. But God has made me small so I can squeeze into the tiny places of people's hearts. The areas so small and hidden, the forgotten stuff in the crevices of the soul. And the big people can take ownership of conference rooms in a heartbeat, but they sure can't fit into the crevices. So we'll go on doing good in our own ways, and I'll do my best to remember that being small is a big superpower, too.

Nicole Smolinski

Today I looked in the mirror and saw a human with a fragile heart that often loves too big. Like a little library-heart, one that lends books out frequently and rarely ever gets them back in as good of condition as before. I told her what a painful combination that is. But I hugged her, and reminded her that we are learning, and that while we learn, I'll have the bandages to tape her love-pages back up when she needs me to.

IV. Autumn

Autumn has rejuvenated me.
Because when I was too overwhelmed,
I felt the crisp breeze
and watched it whisk away
the leaves on the trees above.
Heaviness flew off of them,
and the burdens off my shoulders followed.

Finding My Way Back

Sometimes things are really good and really bad all at the same time. As if our hearts are shape shifting like water around rocks, trying to find the perfect fit amongst the uncomfortable thing we call life. The good news is that if we miss the mark the first time, we are a collection of continuous waves— fueled by a powerful Ocean. We are made to try again.

My choice between anger and grace is a daily one.

And Still

I want to remind myself
That we can grieve what's been taken
and still honor what remains.
That we can let our hearts break
for the suffering that has hit our world
and still stay hopeful for what's to come.
That we can help ourselves
and still help others.
Perhaps our strength
does not look like one
or the other
but instead is an honest mix
of both:
It is a cupped hand
holding grief and gratitude,
self and other,
heartbreak and hope.

Nicole Smolinski

Lately I've realized how much we tend to lose ourselves in the pressures of our every day lives. Culture, people, expectations. Somehow, in our desperate attempts to feel accepted or normal, we lose sight of our value.

The irony is, the more we let go, the more we find what we've been searching for all along. The more we let go of expectations and pressures to be a certain way, the more time we have to just be. The harder I fight to swim, the more I prevent myself from being able to float.

I don't completely understand the ins and outs of this paradox, but I don't think God wants us to go crazy trying to grasp it all. I am learning how to just be, to just rest, and trust that the water will catch me, that I will not drown.

Please don't ever forget that you feel most alive
when you breathe in the small things.

Please don't
ever forget
that you feel
most alive
when you breathe in
the small things.

Most of the time, feeling small is tortuous. Like I'm just a blip in this giant world that can't afford to wait up for me. And so life passes me by. But at times, feeling small is liberating. I am just a blip in this giant world— and so are my struggles. The world cannot afford to wait up for my struggles. And so life swallows them up, gifting me with a blank slate to work on, towards greater joy tomorrow. Only when I remember this does my soul feel biggest.

Nicole Smolinski

Pen hits paper,
And I can breathe again.

In and out like the tide, we are given gifts and they are taken away. We enjoy moments while we can because we know these things are not forever. This shouldn't make us discouraged by what we don't have, but instead push us to be present and grateful in what we do have. There is beautiful humility in this tide-like life.

Sometimes the only thing we can do with our broken heart is to let it break and share it with our Creator— like the communion of sorrow— and hope He knows what to do with our delicate, pained pieces.

Finding My Way Back

Dearest self,
There will be bad days and there will be good days.
You will weep for the bad ones and smile for the good
ones. And you'll continue on. And so it goes.

Dearest self,
There will be bad days and
there will be good days.
You will weep
for the bad ones and
smile for the good ones.
And you'll continue on.
And so it goes.

Finding My Way Back

I hear the storm. The pounding rain, the booming thunder. But I can still remember the silence under the water. There, immersed, I find peace. There is no manual to this life we get. We start, we learn, we conquer. And the next thing you know, it's time to start all over again. I hear the storm. The pounding doubts, the booming fears. The "will you be enough's". But I can still remember it all silenced under the water. There, immersed in grace, I find peace. I invite the storm, because I am brave enough to start again.

Nicole Smolinski

On Waiting

Waiting and growing are not mutually exclusive.
Like a child in the womb prepares for birth,
she waits inside her safe vacuum,
gaining strength for when it's time
to enter this big, unpredictable world.

Finding My Way Back

Today I learned that grass isn't just leftover space on a farm. Cows eat the grass, signaling the plant to release carbon into the soil, which creates new growth and healthy soil all over again. So what seems not tended to is actually the redemption of the farm.

I think our Creator is pretty smart like that too... I think Mother Earth has a sense of humor to use even the tiniest details or quirks to redeem big things and impact people in the most unique of ways.

If you feel out of place on the farm, be encouraged — you're made to look different, made to work humbly behind the scenes, made to be the redemption.

If life feels messy, you're headed in the right direction.

If life feels messy,
you're headed in
the right direction.

I know me best.

I used to be angry at others
for trying to tell me who I am.
Now I'm more angry at myself
for ever believing them.

Finding My Way Back

I am thankful for the Gardener...
who tends to the greenhouse of my soul
and gives me comforting butterfly kisses when I'm
down.

Nicole Smolinski

If waves have ups and downs in their flow,
I think I can allow myself to.

Finding My Way Back

I really don't know

Sometimes people look to me for answers
that I do not have.
And so I tell them to laugh
because we're all just figuring it out
as we go.

Someone told me the other day that it seems like the world hasn't gotten a hold of me yet. But I can't help but think it's the opposite that's made me the way I am now.

I am tired of running circles around my problems when the best way is to limp and crawl straight through them. I've begun to allow the world to get to me just enough to do its job, allow it to bend me and bruise me — allow it to hurt when it should hurt so that I can fully allow myself to heal.

No one invites the pain the world brings, but pain is inevitable at some point in our fallen world. When you let yourself accept the terrifying things that lie inside the lion's mouth, you exit its jaws realizing that you are still alive and grateful for it.

Run the race set before you, even if your race looks like a straight shot into some of your deepest insecurities and wounds. Lean in, face your lions, acknowledge that it's hard, and keep your mind set on what is Good. That is how the lion-world does its full work, if you allow it to.

I am tired of running

circles around my

problems when the best

way is to

limp and crawl

straight through them.

Once you start seeing failure as advice
on how to succeed next,
you have nothing left to lose.

Finding My Way Back

You cannot control
the soil you were planted in,
but you can learn
how to face the sun.

You can not
control the soil you
were planted in
but you can learn
how to face
the sun.

Finding My Way Back

Renovations

I am a big tangled mess of confidence and fear all entwined together. Some days I wake up feeling like I'm finally becoming familiar with the world, like I've finally lived in the big city long enough to know its streets and shortcuts. Like I'm finally feeling like a local.

Other days, I wake up and think about all the tiny shops I've yet to visit and how I still can't remember the best shortcut through crowded areas.

I feel like a tourist in my own body, and I chastise myself for being back here all over again.

Twenty five years seems like a long time to get to know a place, to get to know yourself. But stores in big cities change often and construction redirects your route to work depending on the day and you could be a local of 25 years in a crowded city and still never be able to predict what will happen.

I've been living in my city-body for almost 25 years now and I still come across days where I feel like a complete tourist, unsure of myself, my decisions, how my brain and soul work. Sometimes I'm even tempted to wish some shops inside were different.

123

Nicole Smolinski

That maybe I could be less sensitive or more "life of the party."
That I'd enjoy big exciting clubs rather than the big exciting feeling of looking at the expanse in the night sky.

I sometimes wish I could know every street corner of my soul by name and could choose every single shop inside my city.

But we are plastic people who evolve like any smart city will. Character gets tested, and we must reconstruct it like old buildings needing a retouch. We learn more about the world and how we exist in it.

Things change, and we must constantly relearn the back streets of our city-self. It is exhausting at times, but I guess that's the price we pay for living in a vibrant city rather than a stagnant one.

We are confusing, chaotic, vibrant, alive cities — the days we feel more like tourists than locals are not days to feel defeated, they are days to celebrate renovations.

New Wine

We are crushed and pained by life's hand.
We withstand the pressure.
We wait and wait
until it seems like nothing good will ever come.
And just then, we are new.

Acknowledgements

Thank you to my friends and family who have supported my writing journey over the years. I began years ago as a girl who writes, but your constant encouragement has made me a writer.

Thank you to all the people I've met along the way who've shown me what it is to be truly authentic. Across continents, cultures, and expectations, I've learned bits and pieces of how we get to exist in the world through you. We may never meet again, nor may you ever read these words, but your stories will live on in me forever.

Thank you to my deepest pain and my harshest critics. You have been my greatest teachers. I have learned what it means to proclaim my worthiness in a world constantly telling us otherwise. I am certain I would not be half the woman I am today were it not for my toughest battles. I would never choose to relive them, but I will always be grateful for their bi-product. I am certain that I now know deep joy because I've known deep pain, not in spite of it.

Finally, thank you to my readers. This book wouldn't exist in the same way without eyes to read its pages and souls to experience its story.

About the Author

Nicole Smolinski is a poet, friend, daughter, lover, human, and author of the new collection, *Finding My Way Back*. A marriage and family therapist in training, Nicole writes honestly and vulnerably about pain, joy, wellness and healing in a fantastically difficult world. Nicole received her B.A. in Psychology from the University of California, Davis and is currently in the process of completing her M.S. in Clinical Psychology at Vanguard University of Southern California. Nicole is passionate about living authentically and intentionally. She enjoys using creativity as a channel for cathartic healing with one's self and meaningful connection with others. When not writing or doing clinical work, Nicole enjoys sitting at local coffee shops, eating delicious food with loved ones, and spending time outdoors.

Made in the USA
Coppell, TX
14 February 2022

73604609R00085